SHOHEI OHTANI

★ ALL ACCESS ★

Emma Carlson Berne

Scholastic Inc.

If you purchased this book without a cover, you should be aware that this book is stolen property. It was reported as "unsold and destroyed" to the publisher, and neither the author nor the publisher has received any payment for this "stripped book."

Copyright © 2025 by Scholastic Inc.

All rights reserved. Published by Scholastic Inc., *Publishers since 1920.* SCHOLASTIC and associated logos are trademarks and/or registered trademarks of Scholastic Inc.

The publisher does not have any control over and does not assume any responsibility for author or third-party websites or their content.

No part of this publication may be reproduced, stored in a retrieval system, or transmitted in any form or by any means, electronic, mechanical, photocopying, recording, or otherwise, or used to train any artificial intelligence technologies, without written permission of the publisher. For information regarding permission, write to Scholastic Inc., Attention: Permissions Department, 557 Broadway, New York, NY 10012.

This unauthorized biography was carefully researched to make sure it's accurate. This book is not sponsored by or affiliated with Mr. Ohtani or anyone involved with him.

Photos ©: cover: AP Photo/Ashley Landis; Insert: 1: Jim McIsaac/Getty Images; 2 top: Kyodo via AP Images; 2 bottom: Chung Sung-Jun/Getty Images; 3 top: Kyodo News Stills via Getty Images; 3 bottom: Gregory Shamus/Getty Images; 4 top: Sean M. Haffey/Getty Images; 4 bottom: Sarah Stier/Getty Images; 5: Kyodo via AP Images; 6 top: Allen Berezovsky/Getty Images; 6 bottom: Kyodo via AP Images; 7 top: Harry How/Getty Images; 7 bottom: Allen J. Schaben/Los Angeles Times via Getty Images; 8 top: Daniel Shirey/MLB Photos via Getty Images; 8 bottom: Robert Gauthier/Los Angeles Times via Getty Images. All other photos © Adobe Stock and Shutterstock.com.

ISBN 979-8-225-01255-7

10 9 8 7 6 5 4 3 2 1   25 26 27 28 29

Printed in the U.S.A.   40
First printing 2025

Series design by Sarah Salomon for The Story Division
Cover and photo insert design by Lynne Yeamans for The Story Division

   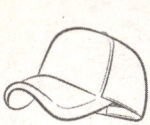

TABLE OF CONTENTS

CHAPTER 1:	*A Rocket? A Jet? A Pitch?*	1
CHAPTER 2:	*The Yakyu Shonen*	8
CHAPTER 3:	*Baseball Genius Develops*	17
CHAPTER 4:	*The Pitch That Changed It All*	29
CHAPTER 5:	*Shohei Turns Pro*	38
CHAPTER 6:	*Shohei, Meet the USA*	48
CHAPTER 7:	*Shohei Struggles*	59
CHAPTER 8:	*Sho-Time*	68
CHAPTER 9:	*Life as a Superstar*	78

CHAPTER 1

A Rocket? A Jet? A Pitch?

Excuse me, was that blur a *pitch*? That's what people in the stands watching the semifinal game between the Ichinoseki Gakuin and Hanamaki Higashi high school teams were thinking. Because on that day—July 19, 2012—Shohei Ohtani had just shown them something *no one* had ever seen before from a high school player.

Shohei was on the mound. He had just turned eighteen. He was six foot four, skinny, and focused like a laser beam. Shohei's face was expressionless as he faced the batter. He bent

over in his stance and nodded at the sign from the catcher. Then the windup—and the pitch.

The batter swiped at it—missed. The clock showed 160 kilometers per hour—95.7 miles per hour. Blistering.

Now the second pitch—the batter jumped back. Ball.

The third pitch, with Shohei lunging forward as he fired the ball at the plate. Strike! 157 kilometers per hour—97.6 miles per hour.

Record-Bashing

The batter grinned, astonished, as if to say, "What, you expect me to *hit* these pitches?" Shohei poised himself again. A moment of stillness as the batter crouched at the plate. Then the windup, fast as a machine, the ball firing, the swing, the miss, then the clock—160 kilometers per hour! 99.4 miles per hour! No one in Japan had ever pitched that fast in a high school game. At seventeen, Shohei Ohtani had set a new record.

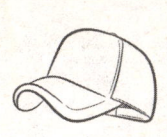

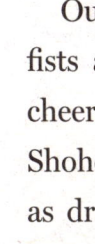

Out on the mound, Shohei clenched his fists and shouted in triumph as the crowd cheered. The batter jogged off the field as Shohei ran in, slapping his teammates' hands as drums beat, the crowd chanted, and the amazed announcers marveled at what they'd just seen.

Rising Up

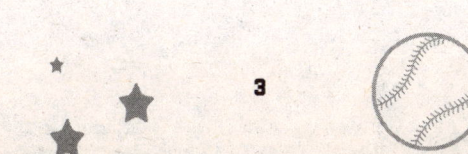

Shohei Ohtani never really left the mound after that day—unless it was to move directly to the batter's box. This left-handed batter and right-handed pitcher now playing in the United States has homered his way to a very small, very elite club made up of the greatest ballplayers ever—Ty Cobb, Willie Mays, and the great Babe Ruth. Whispers float among fans and pros—Shohei Ohtani might be the greatest of all time. From his time as a steel-armed high school player to his record-breaking pro seasons in Japan to his MLB debut—no one has any doubt—Sho-time is here to stay.

FAST FACT

The stadium at Shohei's high school could hold up to 12,000 students—about as big as a minor league baseball stadium in the United States.

ALL ABOUT JAPAN

Shohei loves his home country. Now his fans in the United States can learn to love this vibrant country, too!

- Japan is a string of islands. The four main ones are called Hokkaido, Honshu, Shikoku, and Kyushu. But don't stop there—there are fourteen thousand other tiny islands surrounding these larger pieces of land.

- Four-fifths of Japan is covered with mountains. Climbing trip, anyone?

- Japan is the only country in the world that still has an emperor. Emperor Naruhito took the throne in 2019 after his father stepped down.

Baseball has been played in Japan for over one hundred and fifty years. One of the first introductions to the sport came from an American professor who taught it to his Japanese students in 1872. The first official team was formed in 1878, just six years later. Now it's the country's most popular sport.

Baseball fans in Japan are led by official cheerleaders who wear special robes as they organize cheers. They tell fans which cheer to yell, when to start, and when to stop. Drummers often accompany the cheers.

The first Japanese baseball player to play in MLB was Masanori Murakami, a pitcher who played for the San Francisco Giants in 1964. Murakami took the mound in the eighth inning of the game and received a standing ovation when the inning was over. His hat now resides in the National Baseball Hall of Fame and Museum.

Ready for a snack? At a Japanese baseball game, fans can nosh on *yakitori* (grilled chicken skewers), *takoyaki* (fried octopus balls), *yakisoba* (grilled noodles with toppings), and tiny hot dogs served with ketchup but without buns.

CHAPTER 2

The Yakyu Shonen

Shohei came into the world with athletics in his blood. Born on July 5, 1994, in Mizusawa (now part of Oshu), a city in northwestern Japan, Shohei was the youngest of three children. His dad, Toru, worked at the local Mitsubishi factory and played baseball on the corporate team. His mom, Kayoko, was an Olympic-level badminton player. Now both were focused on raising their children with kindness and sincerity. They didn't want to push their kids too hard. Shohei's big brother Ryuta was sometimes scared to play on the playground equipment in their sleepy rural town. That was okay—Toru and Kayoko didn't push him.

But with Shohei, his parents had a different focus. Shohei was fearless. When his brother would hang back at the playground, Shohei would charge ahead. He would try every piece of equipment—sometimes scaring his parents in the process. "When the switch is turned on, he concentrates and does it all at once, but when the switch is off, he is really off," Shohei's mother said later. "In elementary and junior high school baseball, he would concentrate on practice, but during breaks, he would play more happily than anyone else. He would splash water with his teammates if they had a hose or play golf with a ball and bat."

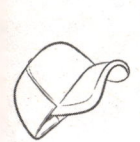

Baseball World

Baseball was what really mattered in the Ohtani family. Ryuta had started playing when he was little, but Toru was often gone for his games and practices, working long hours at the factory. "When Shohei's older brother was playing, I was too busy with work to teach him how to play baseball. I couldn't even play catch with him," Toru said. "Because of that, I was determined to teach Shohei baseball as hard as I could."

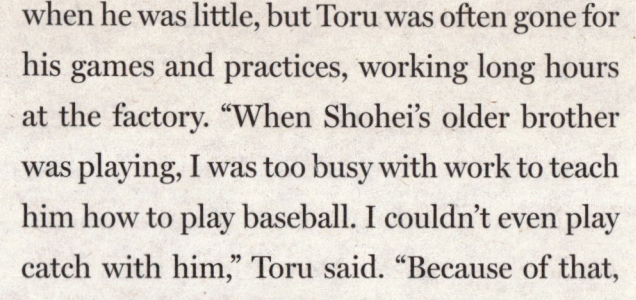

When it was time for Shohei to enter youth baseball, Toru made sure he was around to coach. He showed Shohei how to hit and throw. Later in his life, Shohei remembered that the main lesson he learned from his parents was to follow his heart. "[Baseball] was the first thing I thought looked cool, and I had the most confidence in it," Shohei recalled later. "My mother let me do what I wanted to do as I wanted to do it."

A youth baseball team, the Mizusawa Pirates, practiced near Shohei's house, on a field between a road and a river. One day,

Shohei's parents brought him to meet the coach, Shoji Asari. Shohei wanted to join the team, they explained. He wanted to play baseball.

Coach Asari was concerned. Shohei was very skinny. Wouldn't he rather play softball on his school's team? the coach asked. He knew other kids would be playing on the school team. Shohei would have friends there. Shohei shook his head. No, he said. He wanted to play *real* baseball, right here on this field. It felt right. "I wasn't told to play baseball. I did it naturally," Shohei said years later.

Shohei joined the Mizusawa Pirates and soon people started calling him a *yakyu shonen*—a kid who only thinks of baseball. He watched his favorite Japanese team, the Yomiuri Giants, on TV at night. During the day, he slammed the ball over and over at practice with the Pirates. Even though he was skinny, he could hit balls over the fence and

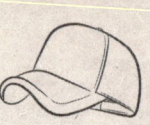

into the river with his powerful left-handed swing. Eventually, the team lost so many balls that Coach Asari told him to start hitting balls into *left* field—opposite-field hitting. Many years later, Shohei would use that same swing to wow outfielders in MLB.

The Two-Sword Style

But the skinny boy from up the road wasn't just a powerful lefty at the plate. He also started pitching—right-handed. This made him a *nitoryu*—a Japanese word that means "two-sword style." Shohei's pitches were diabolical. His curveballs curved. His fastballs blistered over the plate.

But even though Shohei was good—very good—right from the start, that didn't mean his coaches thought he was perfect. Shohei trained hard with the rest of his team, doing repetitive drills like hopping through ladders

laid on the ground. The boys were expected to be obedient and disciplined, or they would be punished—a strict system that was common in Japan during Shohei's childhood.

But even though Coach Asari trained his team hard, he also made sure that Shohei and his teammates had fun on the field. The coach knew that the best baseball skills develop when the players have the chance to be creative. And Shohei loved to play the game—a love he's kept strong throughout his career.

FAST FACT

Shohei learned badminton from his mother when he was just two years old. His favorite part was swinging the racket.

THE BASEBALL BIBLE

Attention, students! Please open your baseball bibles and get to work! Class is now in session.

- People from as far back in history as the ancient Mayans and the ancient Egyptians played games that involved hitting a ball with a stick. But the *modern* sport of baseball was invented over a long period of time in the 1800s. The first official baseball game was played between the New York Knickerbockers and the New York Nines in 1846.

- Today, about seventy-five countries all over the world have professional baseball leagues. The biggest baseball countries are the United States, Cuba, Japan, Canada, the Dominican Republic, and South Korea.

- Before Major League Baseball games, the balls are rubbed with special, secret-recipe mud to help the pitchers get a better grip.

Players in each MLB game use about ninety to one hundred and twenty balls per game. Where do they all go?

Shohei's got some competition! The Guinness World Record for fastest pitch is held by then–Cincinnati Reds pitcher Aroldis Chapman. Aroldis threw this particular streak of fire at a velocity of 105.8 miles per hour on September 24, 2010, in a game against the San Diego Padres.

Batter up! Most MLB baseball bats are made of maple wood. Ash and birch also make good bats!

Wind up—go! Each pitcher only has twelve seconds to pitch the ball after receiving it from the catcher, according to the MLB handbook.

Major league bases are ninety feet apart from one another. A batter can reach first base in about 4.35 seconds.

CHAPTER 3

Baseball Genius Develops

By junior high, Shohei was fourteen years old and six feet tall. He had moved to the Ichinoseki Little Seniors youth team, and Toru was working with him every day. Toru taught Shohei to pitch with his fingers on the seams of the baseball and to hit with the meat of the bat. He insisted Shohei respect his equipment and keep himself and his gear clean and tidy. Shohei was not allowed to throw his mitt or his bat when he was angry. Toru and the other coaches expected Shohei and his teammates to control their emotions.

Toru's coaching was paying off. In a regional championship game, Shohei struck out 17 of 18 batters. At the age of fourteen, he threw an 87-mile-per-hour fastball. By the time he was fifteen? A 95-mile-per-hour fastball. But Shohei didn't consider himself anything special. He didn't think he was good enough to travel for tournaments as other young players did. "I assumed there must be many players better than me," Shohei said many years later.

Staying Near Home

By the time he was finishing junior high, all the high schools in Japan knew about Shohei. He was a phenomenon. And they all wanted him to come and live in *their* city and play for *their* team. But Shohei didn't want to leave home. He wanted to stay in Mizusawa. He picked Hanamaki Higashi High School, in

the town of Hanamaki, about thirty minutes away, and joined the baseball team there.

The program at Hanamaki wasn't just about baseball. The coach, Hiroshi Sasaki, believed the players needed to develop their character as well as their sports skills. He required the players to live in the school's dorms and do chores to keep the buildings neat. Shohei and the other pitchers were assigned to toilet-cleaning duty. Coach Sasaki wanted to remind them that they needed to stay humble on the field and off the field. Since they were the stars on the field, the coach would say, they needed to do the lowest job when they were off the field. Shohei's parents had already taught him the importance of humility and respect. He never complained about the chores, his coach remembered later.

Shohei later recalled how the high school program helped him discipline himself. "I think the environment of the high school

where I lived in the dormitory was . . . good," he said. "I started to think properly before taking action. Even so, I was scolded many times. Once, I was very angry because I overslept. I was taken out of practice for a few days and made to shovel snow. I was the one who had to practice the most on the team, but I created a situation where the head coach had no choice but to do so. I felt bad about that."

Coach Sasaki wanted his players to look inward as well. To do this, the coach used a self-improvement system called the Harada Method. The system asked users to think about five categories: goals, purpose, analysis, plan, and action. Shohei and his teammates had to write down their number-one goal for themselves in baseball. Then they had to write on a grid of squares all the qualities they would need to develop in order to reach that goal. Shohei wrote that he wanted to have "a tenacity for victory" and "a cool head and hot passion."

MLB Dreams

Shohei set his sights high. He wrote that he wanted to be a first-round pick in the Nippon Professional Baseball Draft—Japan's national baseball draft. A couple of years later, Shohei did the exercise again. By now he was seventeen and he had thrown out his old list. Now he'd decided he was going to skip the Nippon Pro Draft altogether and go straight to MLB. Shohei wrote that he wanted to get called up to the major leagues by the time he was twenty. By the time he was twenty-two, he wanted to win the Cy Young Award, baseball's top award for pitching. Shohei wrote that he wanted to win the World Series by twenty-six and play his final game in the majors by forty.

Shohei was still only in high school. No one knew how many of these goals he'd actually achieve. What they did know was that this teenager from Mizusawa was still growing!

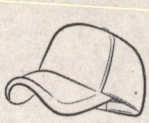

He was six foot four by the time he was a senior. He was also eating up to ten bowls of rice a day in order to pack on the pounds. He cut out junk food and limited his screen time so he could train more. And it worked—Shohei gained forty-five pounds during his high school years.

Even his injuries helped him. When Shohei hurt his hip, he couldn't run. He spent a winter recuperating, eating, and gaining weight—and muscle. Batting was the only practice that didn't hurt—so that's all he did. And he kept getting stronger.

By senior year, catchers were spraining their fingers on his pitches. He was one of the fastest high-school pitchers in Japan. That list he'd made? Check! Check! His trajectory? Rocket-speed straight into the stratosphere.

FAST FACT

In high school, Shohei was also a swimmer. In fact, his coach later said that Shohei could have competed for Japan in the Olympics—he was that good!

FAST FACT

The Harada Method that Coach Sasaki taught to Shohei was created by a Japanese physical education teacher named Takashi Harada.

NOM-NOM!

Shohei knows better than anyone how important a healthy diet is. But sometimes, he indulges in his favorite snacks and drinks.

- Shohei looked very pleased when he was presented with the Japanese gummy candy Poifull by a tween interviewer on the red carpet. The interviewer said she'd heard these candies were his favorite.

- Shohei loves Japanese-style potato chips. They come in flavors like seaweed and honey and butter.

- Shohei told an interviewer that the Japanese snack *takoyaki*—that's fried octopus balls to you—was one of his favorite junk foods. Dodger Stadium added it to their concessions so fans could eat like Shohei.

Shohei is a brand ambassador for one of his favorite drinks—the unsweetened bottled green tea Oi Ocha.

Even though he tries to stay away from sugar, Shohei loves the *konbini* crepes that you can buy in Japan at some convenience stores. These thin pancakes are made with rice flour, then filled with smooth chocolate and rolled up for easy snacking. Mmm!

BUY THIS

Shohei promotes earbuds, watches, pillows, and sneakers. Read on to find out which other products he's pushing.

- Shohei wears earbuds called Powerbeats Pro 2 in ads that showcase his powerful batting.

- In 2023, Shohei signed an endorsement deal with sneaker and sports gear company New Balance. Now he has his own line of clothing and cleats there.

- The star plays casual sandlot baseball with grinning children in a Japanese ad for the software company Salesforce.

- The limited-edition Seiko watch that Shohei endorses has a face that's Dodger blue and a band signed by the star.

- Shohei shows off his smooth skin in an ad campaign for Japanese cosmetic company Kosé.

- The Japanese Internet job agency DIP saw its profile and its stock rise after Shohei became the brand ambassador in 2022.

- The star has had a relationship with the Japanese bedding company Nishikawa since 2017 and still sleeps on one of their custom pillows.

- In 2021, the massive sports memorabilia company Fanatics signed an exclusive deal with Shohei to distribute his autographs.

Shohei Ohtani at bat during the deciding game of the 2024 World Series.

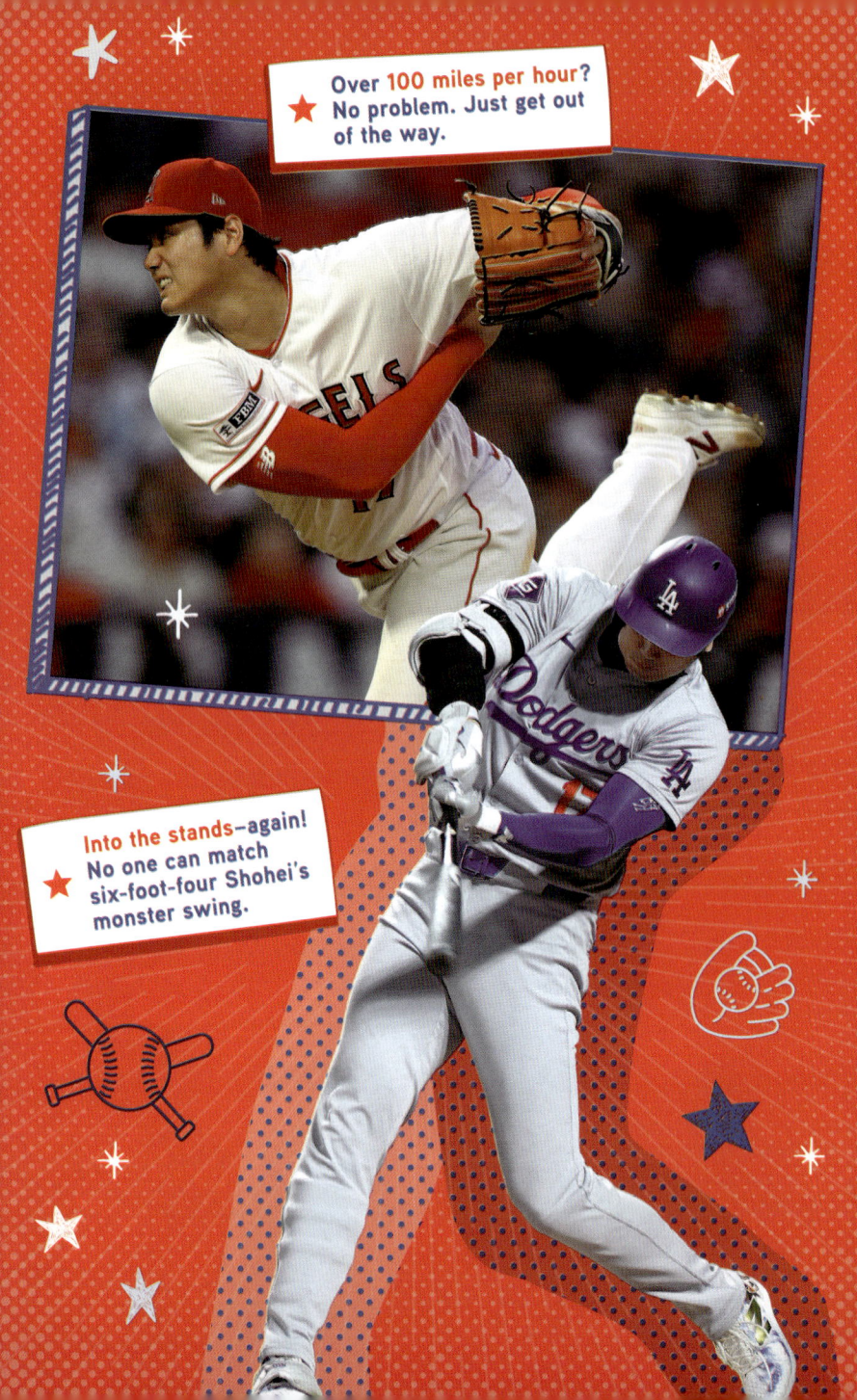

Shohei loves meeting his fans. He surprises a thirteen-year-old pediatric heart patient with a meet-and-greet.

Shohei's wife, Mamiko, understands the athletic life. She was a professional basketball player in Japan.

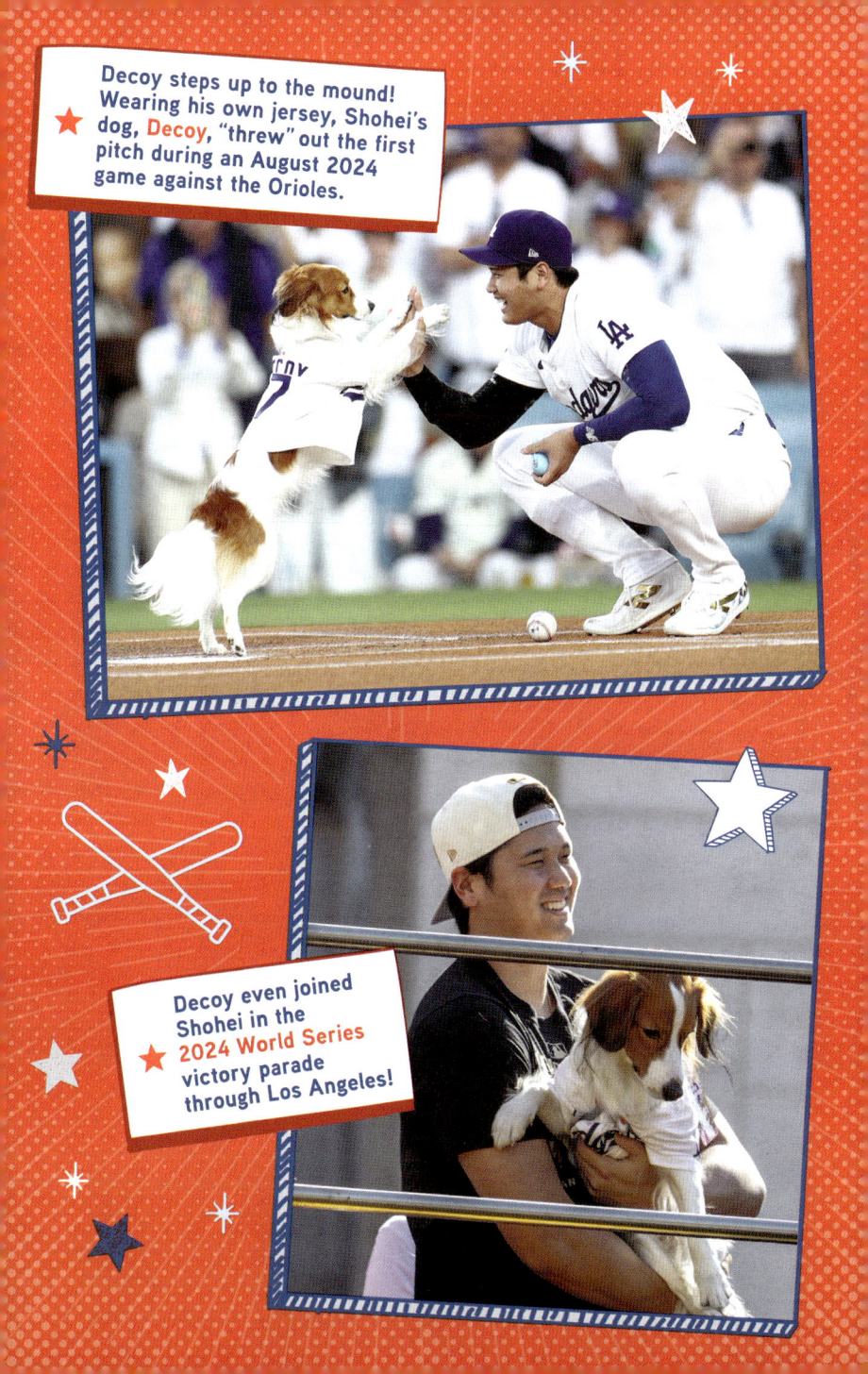

Decoy steps up to the mound! Wearing his own jersey, Shohei's dog, Decoy, "threw" out the first pitch during an August 2024 game against the Orioles.

Decoy even joined Shohei in the 2024 World Series victory parade through Los Angeles!

Never enough Decoy! Shohei shows off his dog-printed suit during the 2024 All-Star game.

World Series winner! Shohei celebrates with his team during their 2024 triumph.

CHAPTER 4

The Pitch That Changed It All

Shohei had never given up on his MLB dreams. He was eighteen years old, he was almost done with high school, and he was determined to go to the United States to play Major League Baseball. After all, the US was the biggest baseball market in the world.

Many Japanese players, especially right out of high school, would first go through the Nippon Pro Draft, the Japanese baseball draft, and play for a Japanese professional team before heading to the United States. But Shohei didn't think he needed to make that decision. After the game against Ichinoseki Gakuin, MLB scouts started taking notice of the six-four teenager with the killer arm. The Boston Red Sox, the New York Yankees, the Texas Rangers, and the Los Angeles Dodgers came knocking at Shohei's door.

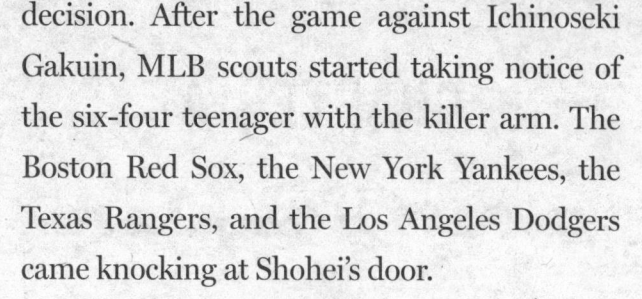

Shohei's pitching was turning heads. But his hitting wasn't impressing every scout. One MLB scouting report said that Shohei was "basically like a high-school hitter." He probably wouldn't be able to hit MLB pitches, the report went on to say.

Draft Refuser

Still, Coach Sasaki encouraged Shohei to go straight to MLB, and the star player agreed. By October 2012, Shohei declared that he had decided to sign with an MLB team. He didn't have a specific team in mind—instead, he was keeping the Nippon Pro from drafting him.

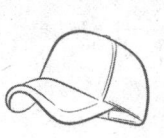

"Great players from every country go [to the US]," Shohei said at the press conference. "I don't want to lose to those players."

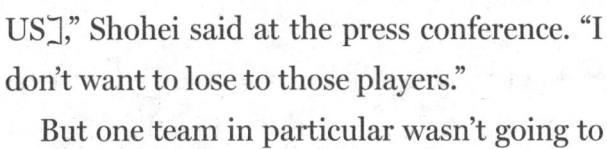

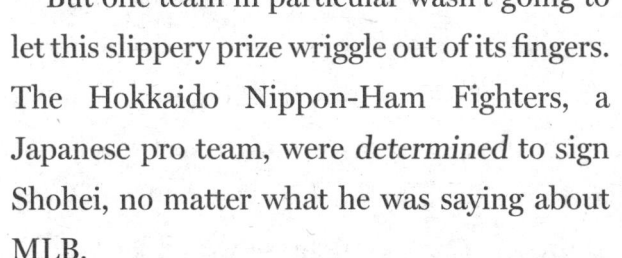

But one team in particular wasn't going to let this slippery prize wriggle out of its fingers. The Hokkaido Nippon-Ham Fighters, a Japanese pro team, were *determined* to sign Shohei, no matter what he was saying about MLB.

So the Fighters mounted a full-on "Shohei in Japan" campaign. Their manager and scout reminded Shohei that he'd enter MLB in the minor leagues, not the majors. He might have to live in a small town on very little money and travel long distances to games. They displayed stats that showed that Japanese players who started in Japan were more successful when they did move on to MLB. He'd start off at the highest level, the Fighters said—no languishing in the minors. Let us draft you, the Fighters said, and we'll make your life very easy.

Two-Way Promises

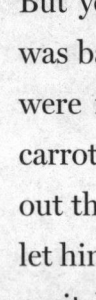

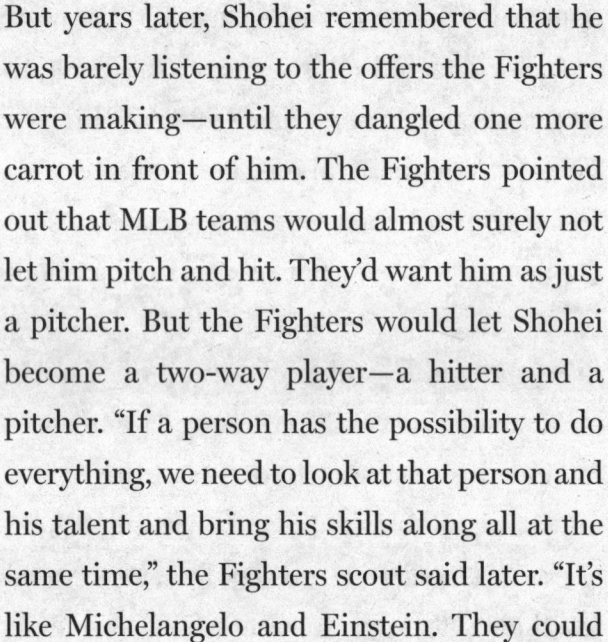

But years later, Shohei remembered that he was barely listening to the offers the Fighters were making—until they dangled one more carrot in front of him. The Fighters pointed out that MLB teams would almost surely not let him pitch and hit. They'd want him as just a pitcher. But the Fighters would let Shohei become a two-way player—a hitter and a pitcher. "If a person has the possibility to do everything, we need to look at that person and his talent and bring his skills along all at the same time," the Fighters scout said later. "It's like Michelangelo and Einstein. They could do art and science, everything."

Shohei hadn't said much to the Fighters up to this point. He had just listened politely. But the chance to dominate behind the plate and on the mound was just too tempting. The

Fighters had won this bout. Shohei entered the Nippon Pro Draft, and the Fighters scooped him up. Shohei was playing the long game with his MLB dreams—and the Fighters were first up to the plate.

FAST FACT

At first, Shohei's father wanted to name him Yoshitsune after a great samurai. But he changed his mind, not wanting his son to feel pressure to live up to this name!

FANS LOVE SHOHEI

Shohei loves baseball, and his fans love Shohei. Read on to see how some of them express their devotion.

- Want to shake Shohei's famous hand? There's a plaster replica of it outside City Hall in Shohei's hometown of Oshu, Japan. You can buy special Shohei wind chimes, too—sold by the Shohei cheer club.

- The Shotime Korea fan club sometimes waits at airports when Shohei is expected to pass through, hoping to catch a glimpse of the star.

- When the Shohei bobblehead went on sale in August 2024, some fans lined up ten hours before the first pitch just to snare one. Later, some bobbleheads showed up on online marketplaces selling for up to $17,000!

- The official Shohei Ohtani fan club in Canada has over 50,000 members and sells T-shirts, buttons, and candles.

- A superfan in Oshu, Japan, has collected about 300 pieces of Shohei memorabilia. He displays them at the hair salon he owns.

- Shohei became the first MLB player to hit 50 home runs in one season in September 2024. The ball landed in the stands (of course) and fans pushed, shoved, and fell on top of one another to try to snare the prize. Later, the fan who wound up with the ball said he was keeping it rather than selling it.

- A nine-year-old LA Dodgers fan stole Halloween when he dressed up like Shohei (who else?), surrounded by a cut-out cardboard box designed to look like a Shohei baseball card.

- During Shohei's first World Series in 2024, fans from Japan bought more tickets to the game than from any other country outside of North America.

SHOHEI SPEAKS

Japanese, English—no matter which language Shohei speaks, he always makes sure he gets heard.

- "They share the same passion with me, a vision and history about winning."—after signing with the Los Angeles Dodgers

- "I'm a student of the game, so I do feel like I need to grow every year, and I think I've been able to do that."—after winning the 2021 AP Male Athlete of the Year Award

- "I feel like I can't be doing the same thing as last year, to have the same stats as last year . . . I need to get better and keep on improving, so that's the plan."—after his 2021 season

- "I'm honored to be able to be part of a season where we played the longest, and to be able to get to know this team . . . My first year and experience winning a World Series has been a tremendous honor."—after leading the Los Angeles Dodgers to a 2024 World Series win

CHAPTER 5

Shohei Turns Pro

Shohei was a pro baseball player now, and only the second Japanese player to get drafted right out of high school as a two-way player. The last guy to perform this feat went pro in 1951. On Opening Day in 2013, the Fighters' newest rookie took the field—not pitching, not quite yet—but playing outfield *and* getting two hits and an RBI on his first day.

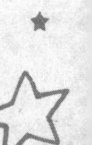

Shohei settled into his rookie season. In the mornings, he'd work out with a minor league team nearby. Nights, he'd play for the Fighters. He finally took the mound as a pitcher in May. The Fighters' marketing team handed out certificates to fans attending that night—this was a historic event.

But Shohei, it turned out, was actually a human player, not a god. He had an okay game—not historic, not awful. He gave up two runs and allowed six hits—fine by most standards, but disappointing for his much-anticipated debut on the mound. In April of his rookie year, he sprained his ankle. That knocked him out for a couple weeks. Then a ball hit him in the face during batting practice, and he fractured his cheekbone. Still, he made the All-Star Game, and his fans loved him, voting him in second for Rookie of the Year.

Full-Time Fighter

But as the first pitch barreled over the plate on Opening Day 2014, a newly healthy Shohei exploded on the field. He was playing with the

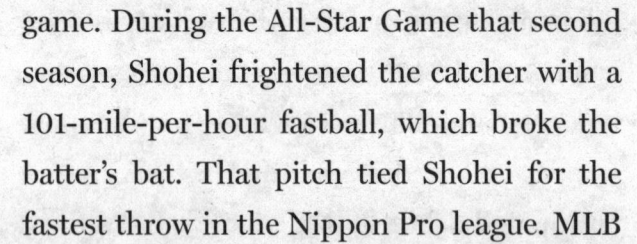

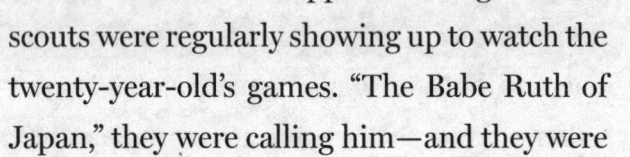

Fighters full time now—no more minor league team in the mornings. His pitching during that second season was the best in the league, averaging about 10 and a half strikeouts per game. During the All-Star Game that second season, Shohei frightened the catcher with a 101-mile-per-hour fastball, which broke the batter's bat. That pitch tied Shohei for the fastest throw in the Nippon Pro league. MLB scouts were regularly showing up to watch the twenty-year-old's games. "The Babe Ruth of Japan," they were calling him—and they were interested.

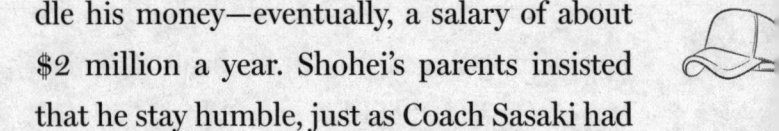

Meanwhile, Shohei was still a *yakyu shonen*—a baseball guy. He tried to think only of his sport. To keep his mind focused, he lived in the team dorms, rather than a glitzy apartment by himself. He let his parents handle his money—eventually, a salary of about $2 million a year. Shohei's parents insisted that he stay humble, just as Coach Sasaki had for so many years. Shohei's mother would only deposit about one thousand dollars a month into his bank account.

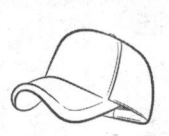

Shohei was taking even better care of his body, too. With nutrition coaching, he switched from white rice to brown rice and stopped eating sugar. He started training not to build muscle, but instead to focus on exploding his hits and runs. He spent almost all his time in the dorm or on the field—no partying, no nightclubs or bars.

Muscle Man

By 2016, Shohei's new nutrition and work-out regimen was showing results. After only two years as a professional player, Shohei was dominant in the league. He nailed 174 strikeouts over 140 innings and only allowed 89 hits over the whole season. He slammed 22 home runs. Pitchers were so afraid of him they'd often just walk him. With Shohei on the mound pitching 102-mile-per-hour fastballs, the Fighters won the Nippon Series championship, making them one of the top teams in Japan.

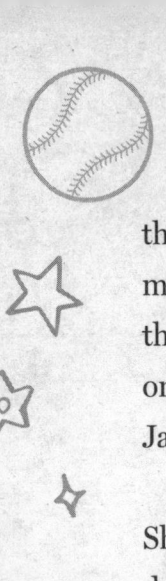

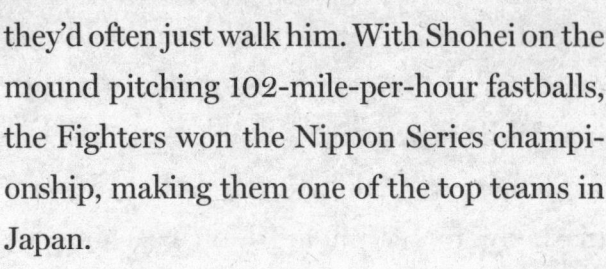

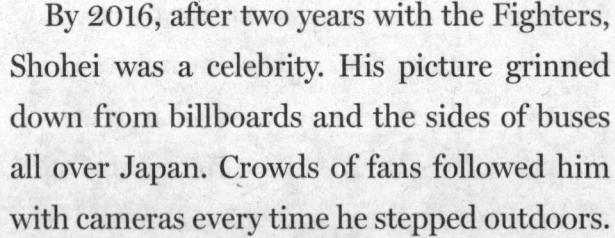

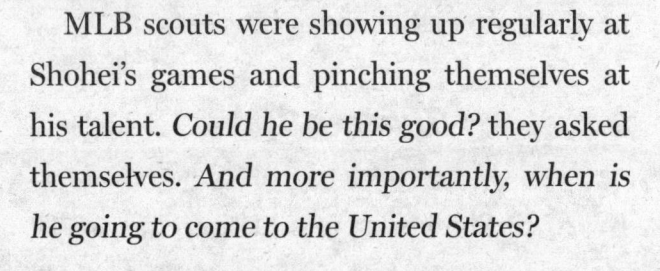

By 2016, after two years with the Fighters, Shohei was a celebrity. His picture grinned down from billboards and the sides of buses all over Japan. Crowds of fans followed him with cameras every time he stepped outdoors.

MLB scouts were showing up regularly at Shohei's games and pinching themselves at his talent. *Could he be this good?* they asked themselves. *And more importantly, when is he going to come to the United States?*

FAST FACT

In November 2016, during the World Baseball Softball Confederation Global Series, Shohei hit a home run that smacked the top of the Tokyo Dome stadium. If it hadn't hit the roof, it was on track to be 525 feet high—that's about as high as a sixteen-story building!

ON THE FIELD

Shohei's greatest moments come when he's doing what he does best—playing ball.

- Shohei reached the famed 50-50 mark in September 2024. Going into the game, he had 49 homers and 50 stolen bases. Then he slammed the ball in the seventh inning against the Florida Marlins, and history was made.

- One of Shohei's signature moves on the field is to step on the base ahead of the base runner, then politely give them a high five. The opposing player always laughs.

- Shohei met legendary Japanese player Ichiro Suzuki on the field during a Los Angeles Angels–Seattle Mariners game and leapt at the chance to shake his hero's hand and offer a polite Japanese bow.

- Shohei surprised a random fan during warm-ups in 2022 when he playfully pitched a ball right at the guy's face. Luckily, he was behind a chain-link fence—that fastball coming at you is no joke.

- Shohei isn't called the best two-way player for nothing. On April 4, 2021, he hit a 115-mile-per-hour home run *and* threw a 100-mile-per-hour pitch in one game.

SHOHEI OFF THE MOUND

Shohei delivers plenty of exciting moments for his fans on the mound—and off as well.

- Shohei shared a great moment with his fellow Japanese player Yoshinobu Yamamoto when the two Los Angeles Dodgers teammates thanked fans for supporting them during their 2024 World Series win.

- Shohei got the news that he was the 2024 MLB Most Valuable Player (his third time) while sitting on his couch at home with his wife, Mamiko, and his dog, Decoy, beside him. His teammate and fellow pitcher Clayton Kershaw delivered the news over video.

When Shohei and Mamiko arrived at South Korea's Incheon Airport to play in the Seoul Series, he was met with fans lining both sides of the hallways, photographers snapping pictures, and plenty of admiring screams. Shohei, wearing headphones around his neck, stayed calm, of course. He had to save his energy for baseball.

In May 2024, Shohei gave thirteen-year-old Albert Lee the surprise of his life when he walked into the Los Angeles Dodgers interview room. Albert, who has had three heart surgeries and now has just half a heart, had no idea he was about to meet his idol. "I couldn't even breathe for, like, thirty seconds," Albert told reporters afterward.

CHAPTER 6

Shohei, Meet the USA

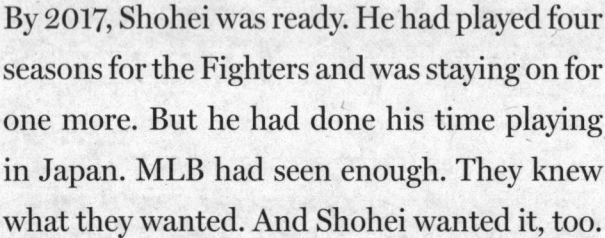

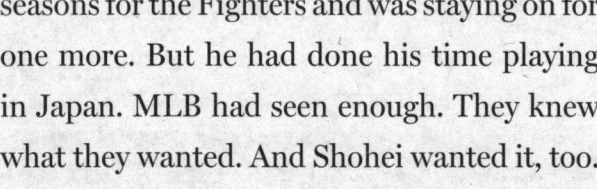

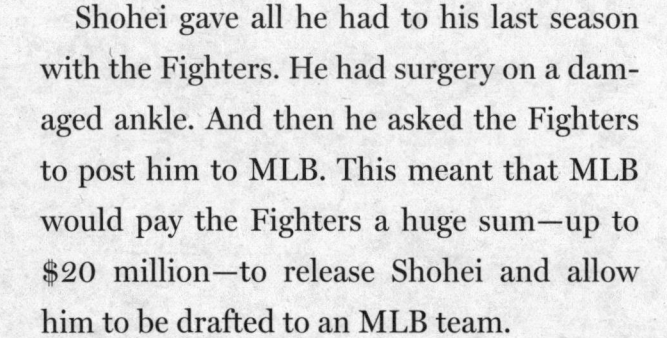

By 2017, Shohei was ready. He had played four seasons for the Fighters and was staying on for one more. But he had done his time playing in Japan. MLB had seen enough. They knew what they wanted. And Shohei wanted it, too.

Shohei gave all he had to his last season with the Fighters. He had surgery on a damaged ankle. And then he asked the Fighters to post him to MLB. This meant that MLB would pay the Fighters a huge sum—up to $20 million—to release Shohei and allow him to be drafted to an MLB team.

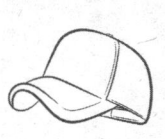

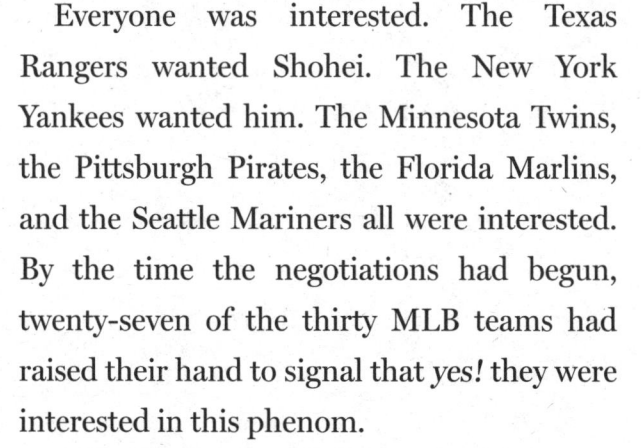

Everyone was interested. The Texas Rangers wanted Shohei. The New York Yankees wanted him. The Minnesota Twins, the Pittsburgh Pirates, the Florida Marlins, and the Seattle Mariners all were interested. By the time the negotiations had begun, twenty-seven of the thirty MLB teams had raised their hand to signal that *yes!* they were interested in this phenom.

Becoming an Angel

Everyone prepared presentations to woo Shohei. In the end, Shohei bypassed the favored New York Yankees and went with the underdog—the Los Angeles Angels. The decision just felt right, Shohei told reporters when he signed. It was a gut thing. "It's hard to explain," Shohei said. "With the Angels, I just felt something click. I'm just glad to make this choice."

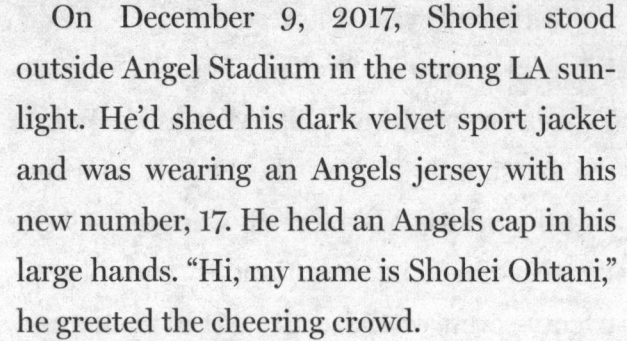

On December 9, 2017, Shohei stood outside Angel Stadium in the strong LA sunlight. He'd shed his dark velvet sport jacket and was wearing an Angels jersey with his new number, 17. He held an Angels cap in his large hands. "Hi, my name is Shohei Ohtani," he greeted the cheering crowd.

"This is a historic day for our organization," Angels manager Mike Scioscia said. "Every player, to a man, is so excited about this acquisition . . . [Shohei's] ability both on the field and in the batter's box is something that doesn't come along—it really never comes along. So our excitement is very, very high."

Shohei was an Angel now. And he was ready to start his life in the USA.

But even though Shohei was living in sunny LA, he still had a lot of pressure to live up to his superstardom. He didn't have time to visit Disneyland or play tourist in California.

Spring training started in two months, and he had to be ready.

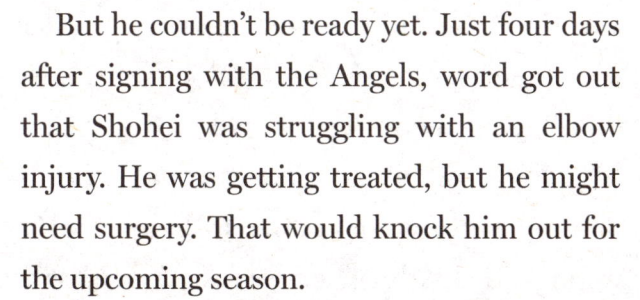

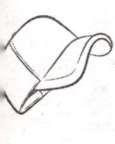

But he couldn't be ready yet. Just four days after signing with the Angels, word got out that Shohei was struggling with an elbow injury. He was getting treated, but he might need surgery. That would knock him out for the upcoming season.

Shohei had to be careful, the Angels management agreed. His elbow was okay *for now*, but he was going to be pitching balls over one hundred miles per hour. That put him at a higher risk for arm and shoulder injuries. And he was going to be pitching every five days as opposed to the every seven days he was used to in Japan. More risk.

Shohei Shows Up

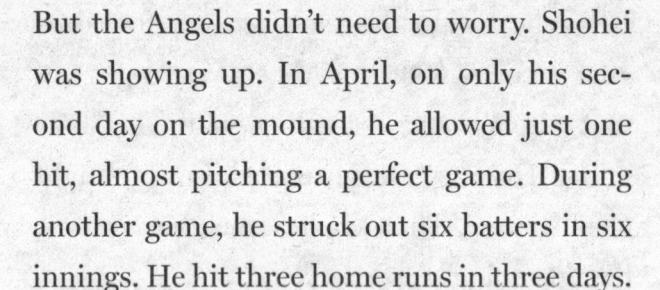

But the Angels didn't need to worry. Shohei was showing up. In April, on only his second day on the mound, he allowed just one hit, almost pitching a perfect game. During another game, he struck out six batters in six innings. He hit three home runs in three days.

And Shohei was having fun off the mound, too. He needed an interpreter to help him with English, but he was enjoying hanging out with his new team. Sometimes they shot baskets or played golf. Shohei went to his first pro hockey game. He played *Clash Royale* with his teammates. Through his interpreter, he learned American trash talk. His teammates even teased Shohei about his fashionable skinny jeans by playing a Japanese pop song called "Fashion Monster" during one of his walk-ups.

Shohei closed out his rookie season with a cherry on top—winning the American League

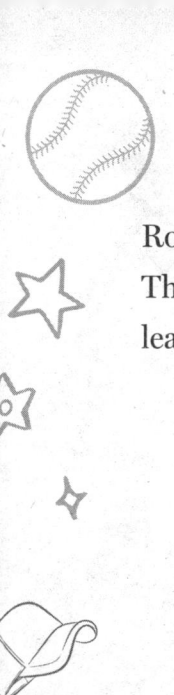

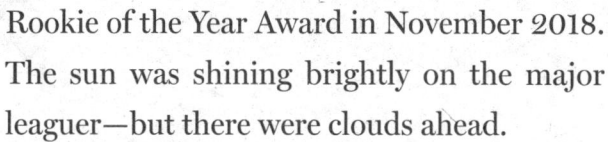

Rookie of the Year Award in November 2018. The sun was shining brightly on the major leaguer—but there were clouds ahead.

FAST FACT

When Shohei signed with the Angels, he joked that he had chosen number 17, but that he'd really wanted number 27—Mike Trout's number.

DECOY THE DOG

Shohei loves baseball—but does he love his dog, Decoy, even more? Read on and decide for yourself!

- Shohei's beloved dog, Decoy, is a brown-and-white ball of cuteness, a Dutch kooikerhondje. This sporty, medium-sized dog has a flowy, silky coat. Decoy is athletic, friendly, and loves to play ball—just like his owner!

- The kooikerhondje was originally bred to hunt ducks. They were supposed to herd the ducks into canals covered with nets so hunters could shoot them.

- Decoy sometimes takes the mound, too, just like Shohei. In August 2024, the little dog "threw" out the first pitch in front of 54,000 fans during a Dodgers game against the Baltimore Orioles, wearing his own little jersey. He didn't even look nervous.

- When the Dodgers held their World Series victory parade in November 2024, the team rode on a double-decker bus. Decoy came along for the ride—on the top of the bus, of course.

- And when Shohei found out that he was the first player in MLB history to be unanimously selected as MVP twice—who was sitting on his lap? If you guessed someone with four feet, a tail, and a pink tongue, you're correct—it was Decoy.

- Sometimes, Decoy likes to dress up. Shohei put him in a fuzzy brown sweater for a walk and a photo shoot the day after winning the 2024 World Series.

- Decoy's name is *actually* Dekopin—a Japanese word that means giving someone a little, playful finger flick to the forehead. Shohei has said that he thought "Decoy" would be easier for Americans to pronounce.

COMING UP TO THE PLATE

Shohei needs music to get him ready for homers. Here are some of his favorite walk-up songs, past and present.

- "Can't Get Enough" by Ghost Machines
- "Do or Die" by Afrojack
- "Game of Thrones Main Title Theme" by Ramin Djawadi
- "Fashion Monster" by Kyary Pamyu Pamyu
- "Twinbow" by Slushii and Marshmello

- "Lost in Paradise" by Ali and AKLO
- "The Show Goes On" by Lupe Fiasco
- "Life in the Fast Lane" by The Eagles
- "Love Rockets" by The Birthday
- "Il Vento d'Oro" (from *JoJo's Bizarre Adventure*) by Yugo Kanno
- "The Greatest Show" (from *The Greatest Showman*) by Benj Pasek and Justin Noble Paul

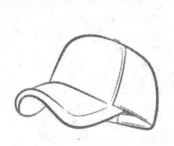

CHAPTER 7

Shohei Struggles

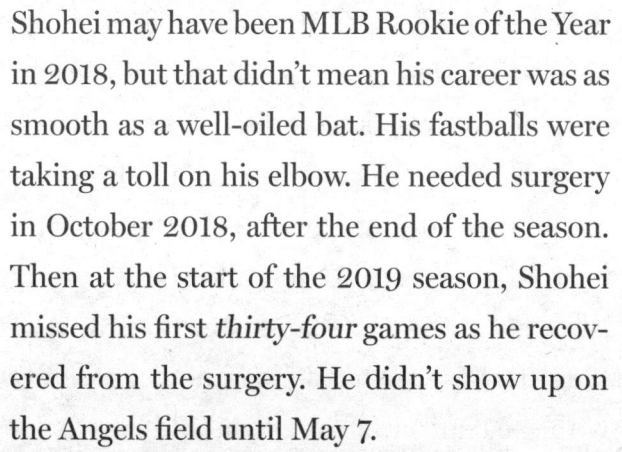

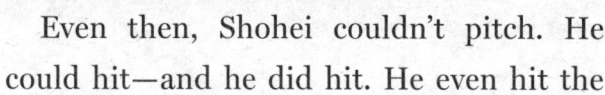

Shohei may have been MLB Rookie of the Year in 2018, but that didn't mean his career was as smooth as a well-oiled bat. His fastballs were taking a toll on his elbow. He needed surgery in October 2018, after the end of the season. Then at the start of the 2019 season, Shohei missed his first *thirty-four* games as he recovered from the surgery. He didn't show up on the Angels field until May 7.

Even then, Shohei couldn't pitch. He could hit—and he did hit. He even hit the cycle in June, smashing a single, a double, a triple, *and* a homer in a single game. He was the first Japanese-born player to accomplish this feat.

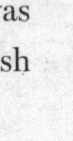

But Shohei's bad season wasn't over. His knee was bothering him. He wanted to push through the injury—he could do it! But the Angels coaches wanted him healthy for the next season. Shohei only played 108 games before he trudged off the field in September. He traded in his jersey for a hospital gown and buckled down for knee surgery and rehab.

Shohei was disappointed. "I felt like I could have put together a lot better season," he told reporters. "I felt like I was going through struggles that lasted a little too long. It wasn't what I imagined, especially with the team situation. It should have been a lot better."

Plagued by Injury

When COVID-19 arrived in spring 2020, Major League Baseball shut down along with the rest of the world. Shohei spent his days rehabbing his elbow. When baseball started back up again, he wanted to be ready. In July 2020, when MLB resumed games for a shortened season, Shohei was on the mound—but only briefly.

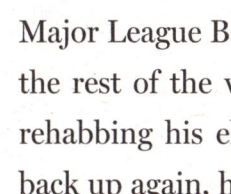

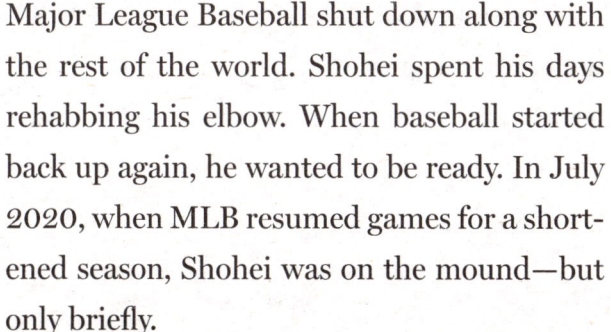

By August, his coaches had pulled him. His throwing arm was hurting him, and everyone was frustrated—Shohei, his coaches, his fans. He had to buckle down to rehab. But the question was starting to come up: Could Shohei stay healthy enough to be the pitcher the world knew he could be? He had the skill, the muscle, the talent, and the nerves. But did he have the joints?

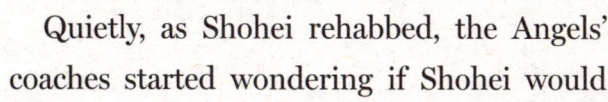

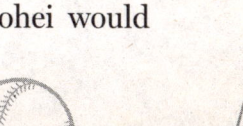

Quietly, as Shohei rehabbed, the Angels' coaches started wondering if Shohei would need to become a position player—first base maybe? Right field?

They had one of the best pitchers in the world—but Shohei needed to show them that his arm was steady and ready. And Shohei was trying to do just that. The question was: Could he?

FAST FACT

During the COVID-19 pandemic, Shohei contributed a signed bat to auction off in order to raise funds to support Japanese healthcare workers.

TRAIN LIKE SHOHEI

Shohei Ohtani didn't get to be one of the best two-way players on the planet by talent alone. He trains hard—here's how he does it!

- Lift heavy weights. In one training video, Shohei deadlifts 550 pounds. Whoa!

- Focus, focus, focus. One Dodgers teammate remembered watching Shohei take twenty practice swings. Each one took him one full minute, because Shohei would visualize his swing and breathe before swinging the bat.

- Don't waste time. Within just two days of signing his new contract with the LA Dodgers in February 2024, Shohei was down in Arizona at the Dodgers' spring training stadium, working out on the field.

- Take your warm-up seriously. Shohei uses a special kind of weighted baseball along with a small radar device to warm up before games. These little technological tweaks help him use his muscles and energy as efficiently as possible.

- Start young. In high school, Shohei and his teammates would start practice every morning after a six o'clock wake up, then go to classes, then practice again until nine or ten at night—every day.

- Diet is key. Shohei saw big improvements in his game when he switched from white rice to brown, started eating oatmeal, and cut out sugar.

- Don't forget protein to build lean muscle! Shohei eats plenty of chicken and fish for lean protein. He consumes about 30 grams per meal—most people eat 30 grams per *day*.

SHOHEI LOVES . . .

Mostly baseball and his dog, but there's a few other things that make the list.

- His house. In 2023, Shohei bought a midcentury-style home in a neighborhood about eleven miles from Dodger Stadium. The $8 million house has a pool (of course), a home gym, a home theater, and a sauna. But sadly, Shohei never actually got to live in the house. After the address got out, too many reporters showed up to take pictures.

- In-N-Out Burger. Shohei has said that the California fast-food chain is his favorite.

- His portable ice machine. Shohei needs to ice his muscles on the regular, and this boom box–sized gadget makes sure he has the cold stuff wherever he goes.

Manga! These Japanese-style comics are wildly popular around the world—and Shohei has said that the sports manga *Slam Dunk* is a personal fave.

Clash Royale. Shohei dominated the Angels clubhouse when he and his teammates went head-to-head on this video game.

His special pillow. The Japanese bedding company Nishikawa took measurements of Shohei's head and shoulders, then made him a custom cushion. It even comes with its own travel bag!

His dog, Decoy. Shohei often posts Instagram shots of the little hound cuddling on couches and beds or walking on a leash in the autumn leaves.

His wife. Shohei married Japanese basketball player Mamiko Tanaka in February 2024.

His iPad. The athlete uses it to organize his practice schedule, diet, and stats.

And of course—his bat! Shohei's favorite bat is made of wood—a type called hard maple, to be exact. His name is written on it in Japanese characters.

CHAPTER 8

Sho-Time

He could. Oh yes, he could. A healthy Shohei exploded onto the field during the 2021 season. His elbow and his knee were finally solid. And he was ready—he was *so* ready. As the spring breezes blew over LA, Shohei was on the mound, pitching, then hitting as the designated hitter in the same game—practically unheard of in the baseball world. He was the designated hitter the day before he pitched, and why not the day after, too?

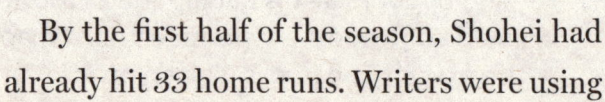

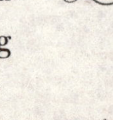

By the first half of the season, Shohei had already hit 33 home runs. Writers were using words like "historic." He became the first Angels player to hit 40 home runs and steal 20 bases in the same season. On July 9, he hit a homer 463 feet—so high into the rafters at T-Mobile Park in Seattle that the TV camera operators couldn't pull back far enough to catch the image of the ball. Instead, fans were looking around, wondering where the ball was.

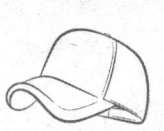

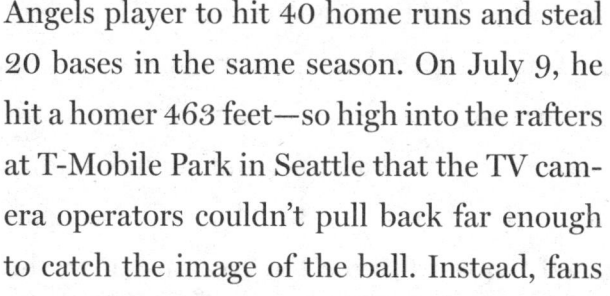

Phenom

By the end of the 2021 season, Shohei became the first player in MLB history to slam 45 homers and steal 25 bases. Pitchers and managers were so scared of him that they regularly walked him to first base, always drawing boos from the crowd, who wanted to see Shohei slam the ball—even from fans on the *other* team!

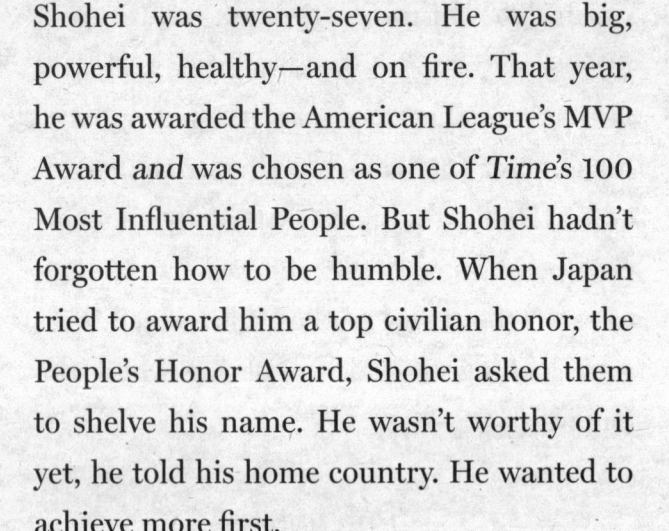

Shohei was twenty-seven. He was big, powerful, healthy—and on fire. That year, he was awarded the American League's MVP Award *and* was chosen as one of *Time*'s 100 Most Influential People. But Shohei hadn't forgotten how to be humble. When Japan tried to award him a top civilian honor, the People's Honor Award, Shohei asked them to shelve his name. He wasn't worthy of it yet, he told his home country. He wanted to achieve more first.

But as far as the Japanese people were concerned, Shohei was already at the top. The skyscraper Tokyo Tower was lit in Angels colors, and Shohei's jersey number 17 was projected onto the side. Japanese fans came to Angel Stadium to hold up signs reading "Ohtaniland."

Japanese fans weren't the only ones filling the stands. The Angels' front office estimated that on the days when Ohtani was pitching, an average of three thousand extra fans filled the stands.

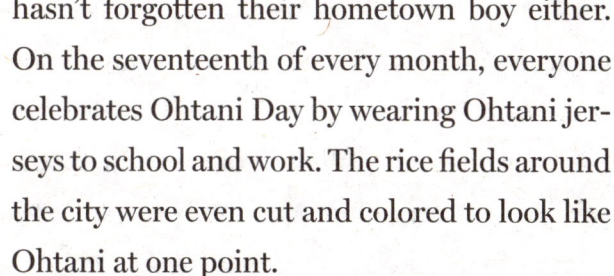

Oshu, the town where Shohei was born, hasn't forgotten their hometown boy either. On the seventeenth of every month, everyone celebrates Ohtani Day by wearing Ohtani jerseys to school and work. The rice fields around the city were even cut and colored to look like Ohtani at one point.

Fun on the Field

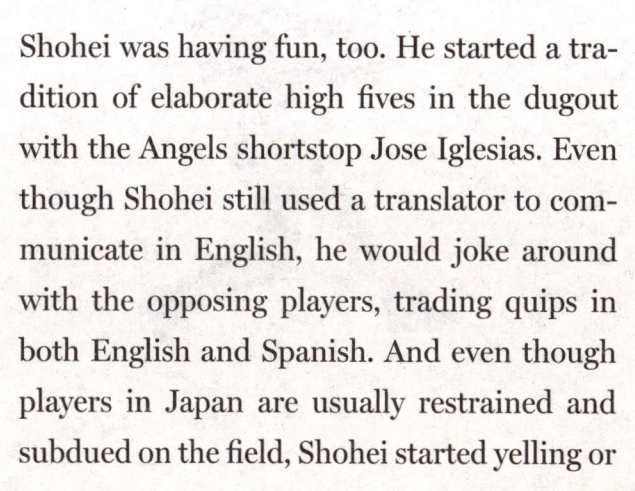

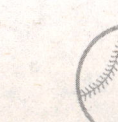

Shohei was having fun, too. He started a tradition of elaborate high fives in the dugout with the Angels shortstop Jose Iglesias. Even though Shohei still used a translator to communicate in English, he would joke around with the opposing players, trading quips in both English and Spanish. And even though players in Japan are usually restrained and subdued on the field, Shohei started yelling or pumping his fist after big hits or big outs—more like his American teammates.

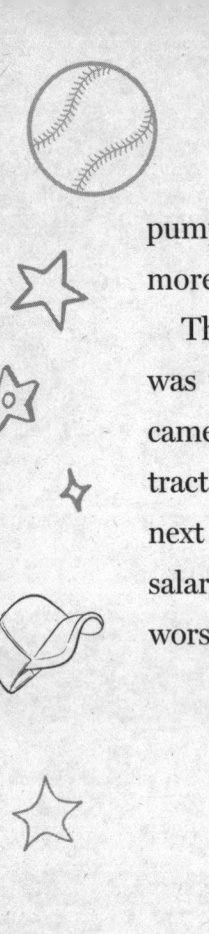

The Angels management agreed that Shohei was worth any price. After the 2022 season came to an end, Shohei signed a new contract with the Angels for $30 million for the next season—$25 million more than his 2022 salary of $5.5 million. But the best—and the worst—for Shohei was yet to come.

FAST FACT

Shohei speaks some English and some Spanish. He occasionally answers questions in English out on the road, but he mainly prefers to speak through a Japanese interpreter.

The Bambino vs. Sho-Time

Shohei has long been compared to The Bambino. He's even been called the "Japanese Babe Ruth." So how do these two-way icons stack up when they go head-to-head?

The Bambino

BIRTH
1895, Baltimore, Maryland, USA

PRO CAREER
Boston Red Sox 1915–1919, New York Yankees 1920–1934, Boston Braves 1934

CAREER HOME RUNS
714

BATTING AVERAGE
342

EARNED RUN AVERAGE
2.28

CAREER BASES STOLEN
123

Sho-Time

BIRTH

1994, Mizusawa (now Oshu), Japan

PRO CAREER

Hokkaido Nippon-Ham Fighters 2013–2017, Los Angeles Angels 2018–2023, Los Angeles Dodgers 2023–present

CAREER HOME RUNS

225 (so far!)

BATTING AVERAGE

.281

EARNED RUN AVERAGE

3.01

CAREER BASES STOLEN

145 (so far!)

GREATEST BASEBALL PLAYERS

Shohei is one of the all-time greats—and he's joining a long line of them! Read on to learn a little more about some of baseball's *other* stars.

- Willie Mays: The New York Giants and Mets center fielder from 1951 to 1973 has been called the greatest all-around ball player ever to have lived.

- Babe Ruth: Shohei has often been compared to The Bambino, who played for the Boston Red Sox and the New York Yankees in the early decades of the 1900s. The Babe is remembered for being one of the greatest two-way players—a lefty pitcher *and* a hitter—just like Shohei.

- Hank Aaron: He broke Babe Ruth's home run record, but more than that, Aaron was a voice for civil rights and spoke out against racism on and off the field.

- Jackie Robinson: The first Black player to play on a major league team, Robinson never let the abuse and discrimination he endured distract him from his goal—playing baseball for the Brooklyn Dodgers.

- Mickey Mantle: He wore New York Yankees pinstripes during his entire eighteen-season MLB career and overcame a shin injury in childhood to be inducted into the Baseball Hall of Fame in 1974.

- Barry Bonds: Pittsburgh Pirates and New York Giants player for 22 seasons, Bonds broke the MLB record for career homers and single season homers.

- Satchel Paige: In 1948, the six-foot-three pitcher for the Cleveland Indians (now the Cleveland Guardians) became the first Black pitcher to take the mound in a World Series.

- Johnny Bench: One of the greatest catchers of all time, Johnny Bench struck fear into the hearts of the batters at his home plate during his seventeen-year career with the Cincinnati Reds.

CHAPTER 9

Life as a Superstar

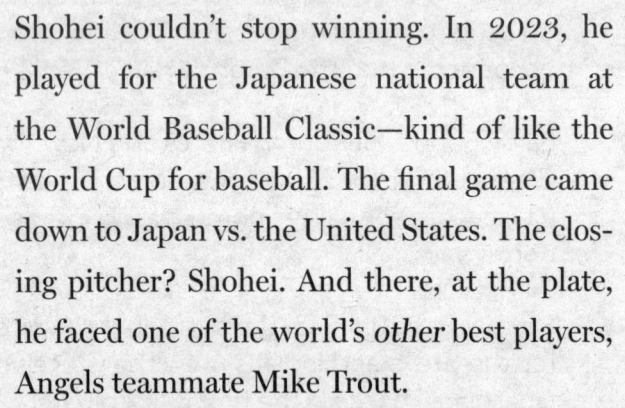

Shohei couldn't stop winning. In 2023, he played for the Japanese national team at the World Baseball Classic—kind of like the World Cup for baseball. The final game came down to Japan vs. the United States. The closing pitcher? Shohei. And there, at the plate, he faced one of the world's *other* best players, Angels teammate Mike Trout.

It was the bottom of the ninth inning and the US had two outs. The score was Japan, 3, the US, 2. All they had to do was get one more player out—and Shohei was on the mound.

Ohtani vs. Trout

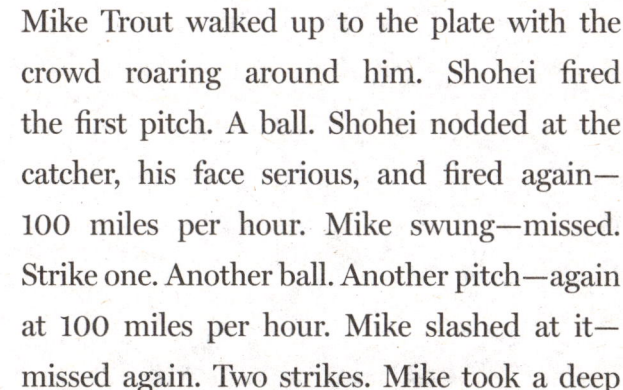

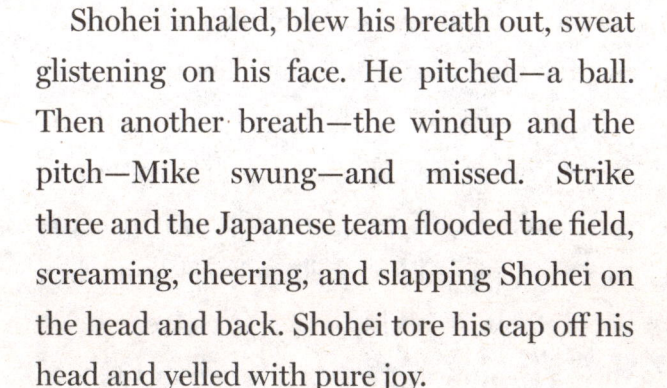

Mike Trout walked up to the plate with the crowd roaring around him. Shohei fired the first pitch. A ball. Shohei nodded at the catcher, his face serious, and fired again—100 miles per hour. Mike swung—missed. Strike one. Another ball. Another pitch—again at 100 miles per hour. Mike slashed at it—missed again. Two strikes. Mike took a deep breath. The crowd was seething with tension.

Shohei inhaled, blew his breath out, sweat glistening on his face. He pitched—a ball. Then another breath—the windup and the pitch—Mike swung—and missed. Strike three and the Japanese team flooded the field, screaming, cheering, and slapping Shohei on the head and back. Shohei tore his cap off his head and yelled with pure joy.

Shohei had loved his time with the Angels, but as the 2023 season drew to a close, he became a free agent. Now he could choose his team from those who wanted him. And everyone wanted him. In the end, Shohei shattered another record in December 2023 when he signed a $700 million, ten-year contract with the LA Dodgers, the largest contract in professional sports history at the time.

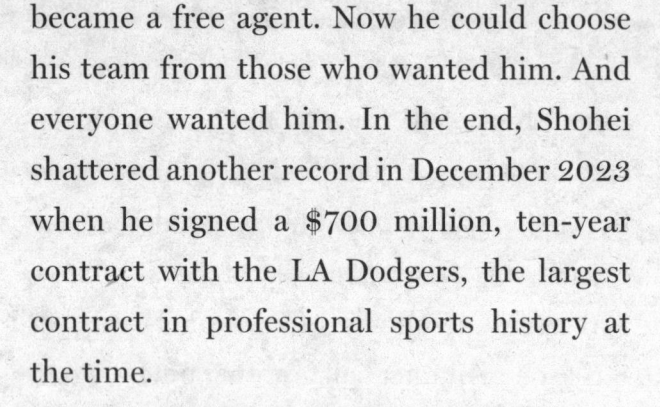

Interpreter Scandal

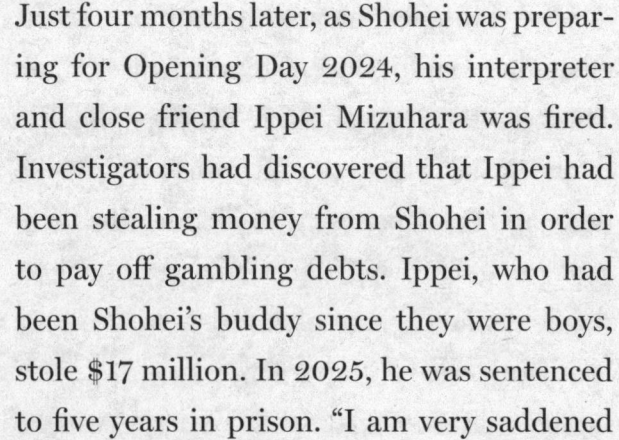

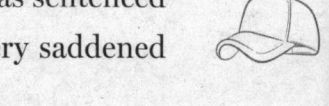

Just four months later, as Shohei was preparing for Opening Day 2024, his interpreter and close friend Ippei Mizuhara was fired. Investigators had discovered that Ippei had been stealing money from Shohei in order to pay off gambling debts. Ippei, who had been Shohei's buddy since they were boys, stole $17 million. In 2025, he was sentenced to five years in prison. "I am very saddened and shocked that someone who I trusted has done this," Shohei said in a statement when the theft was discovered.

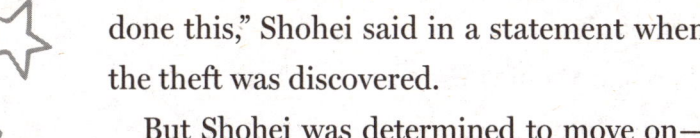

But Shohei was determined to move on—both on and off the field. In September, he became the first person in MLB history to steal 50 bases and hit 50 home runs in one season. And he closed out his 2024 season with a big first—a World Series win, clinching the title 7 to 6 against the Yankees. "I'm honored to be able to be part of a season where we played the longest, and to be able to get to know this team," Shohei told reporters. "My first year and experience winning a World Series has been a tremendous honor."

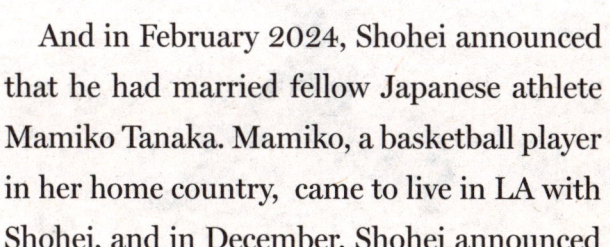

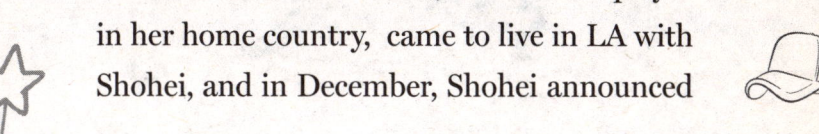

And in February 2024, Shohei announced that he had married fellow Japanese athlete Mamiko Tanaka. Mamiko, a basketball player in her home country, came to live in LA with Shohei, and in December, Shohei announced on social media that they were expecting their first baby.

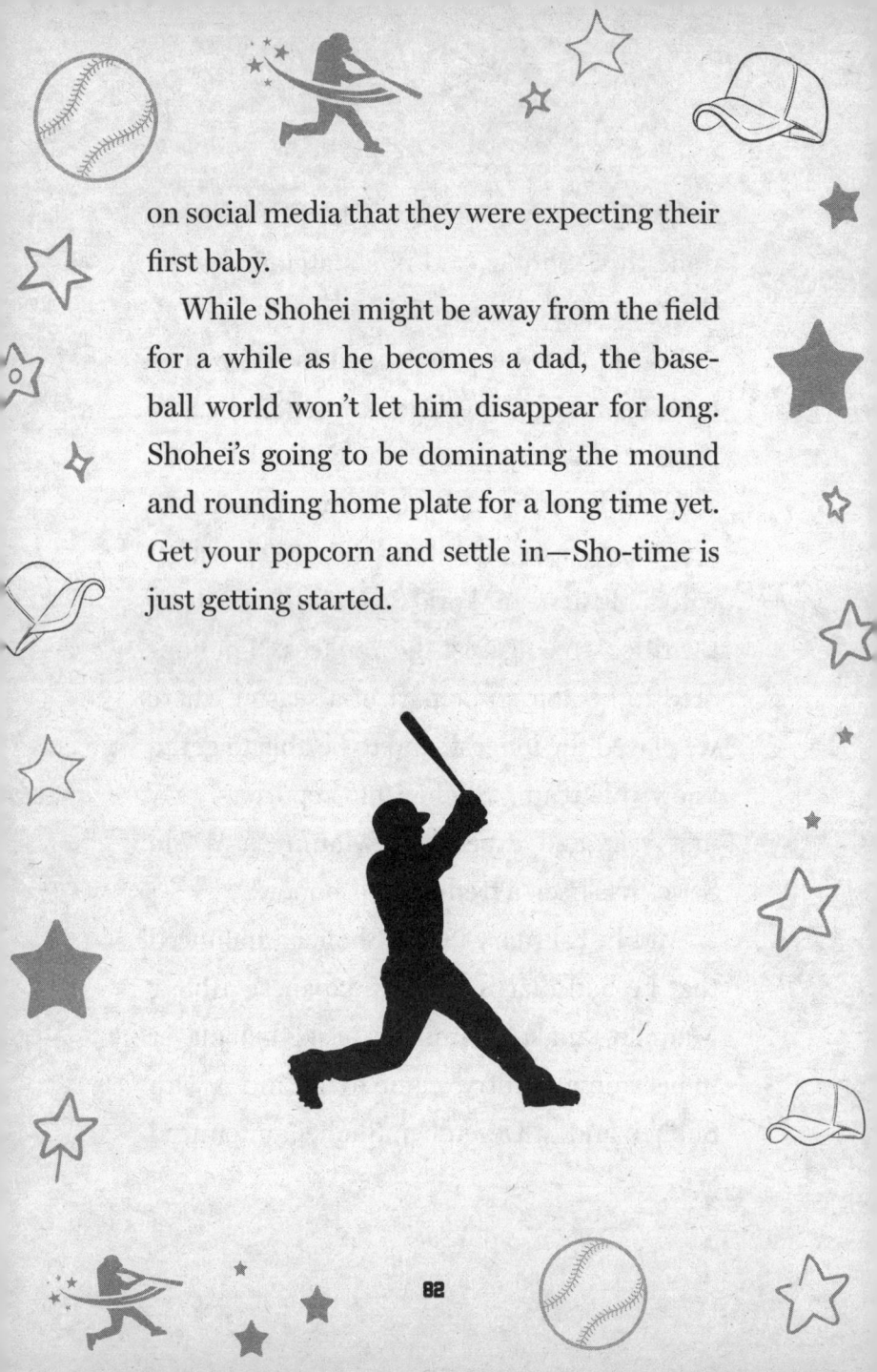

While Shohei might be away from the field for a while as he becomes a dad, the baseball world won't let him disappear for long. Shohei's going to be dominating the mound and rounding home plate for a long time yet. Get your popcorn and settle in—Sho-time is just getting started.

FAST FACT

Shohei uses the same glove for both practices and games. He uses a different model each season.

TALKING ABOUT SHOHEI

Teammates and coaches speak up!

- "His power is enormous. He hit the most majestic homer I've seen in a while. I'm mostly amazed at the ease he plays with. He doesn't try too hard or give the impression that he is stressed physically or mentally. Completely under control."
—**Detroit Tigers manager A.J. Hinch**

- "He's got the best stuff in the league, I think. I don't think I've talked to anybody in the league that wants to face that dude. And at the plate, he's got very little weaknesses."
—**former Angels teammate Mike Trout**

- "He's got a great sense of humor and is always laughing and joking easily."
—**former Angels manager Joe Maddon**

"He kind of reminds you of Nolan Ryan and then he reminds you of freaking Barry Bonds. He's both of those guys. I mean, he's got great stuff and he can hit a home run with the best of anybody. Nobody else has done it before; I mean, the last guy was who, maybe Babe Ruth? Nobody's been able to do that."
—Hall of Fame pitcher Greg Maddux

"We should make a new award for him. This is something MLB hasn't seen since Babe Ruth . . . he's the best player."
—Boston Red Sox manager Alex Cora

"MVP with ease. He should win it every year. What he's doing is insane. All of us at the highest level can't believe our eyes. Truly remarkable. Be thankful you get to witness a real GOAT!"
—New York Yankees pitcher Marcus Stroman

"This guy consumes all things baseball . . . There is not a lot else going on in his world."
—Angels general manager Billy Eppler

SMASHING ALL THE RECORDS

Shohei doesn't just smash balls (and bats)—he smashes records, too!

- In high school, Shohei set a record for the fastest pitch by a Japanese student, clocking in at 99.4 miles per hour. His 2012 record stood for six years, until 2019.

- He was the first MLB player to steal 50 bases and hit 50 home runs in one season. In the end, he actually stole 54 bases and hit 59 home runs.

- Shohei was the first MLB player to pitch more than 100 innings and have 100 strikeouts *and* have more than 100 hits, RBIs, and runs as a batter in a single season.

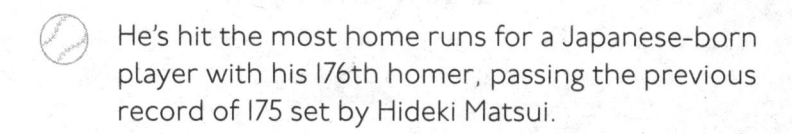

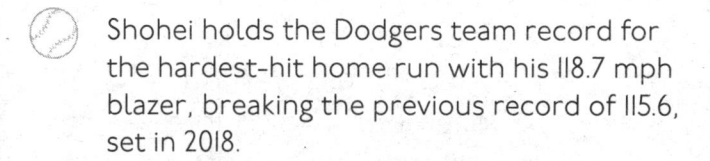

- He's hit the most home runs for a Japanese-born player with his 176th homer, passing the previous record of 175 set by Hideki Matsui.

- Shohei holds the Dodgers team record for the hardest-hit home run with his 118.7 mph blazer, breaking the previous record of 115.6, set in 2018.

TIMELINE

2024

Shohei announces in February that he has married Mamiko Tanaka. In December, the couple reveal they are expecting their first baby. Shohei becomes the first player in MLB history to hit 50 home runs and steal 50 bases in one season and helps the Dodgers to a World Series win.

2023

Shohei pitches for the Japanese national team at the World Baseball Series and leads his country to a championship. He signs a $700 million contract with the LA Dodgers, the largest ever signed in professional sports history. (It has since been surpassed by the New York Mets' contract with Juan Soto.)

2021

Shohei becomes the American League's MVP and is chosen as one of *Time*'s 100 Most Influential People.

2018

Shohei wins the American League Rookie of the Year Award.

2017

Shohei is drafted by the Los Angeles Angels and comes to the United States to play MLB baseball.

2013

Shohei joins the Hokkaido Nippon-Ham Fighters and plays in his rookie season.

2012

Shohei pitches a ball 99.4 miles per hour in a game and sets a new record for Japanese high school pitching.

2010

Shohei enters Hanamaki Higashi High School and joins the baseball team there.

2002

Shohei begins playing Little League baseball with the Mizusawa Pirates.

1994

Shohei is born on July 5 in Mizusawa, Japan.

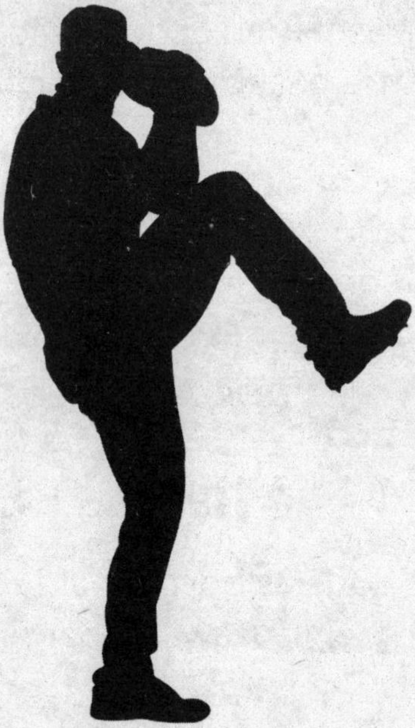